Harai-Goshi

HARAI-GOSHI

JUDO MASTERCLASS SERIES

JEAN-LUC ROUGÉ

Ippon Books

First published by
Ippon Books Ltd
55 Long Lane,
London N3 2HY

British Library Cataloguing in Publication Data

Rougé, Jean-Luc
    Harai-Goshi : Judo masterclass techniques.
    1. Judo
    I. Title
    796.8152

ISBN   1 85223 597 7

Acknowledgements
My first thanks go to my valiant uke, Francois Fournier, and my friend
Jean-Pierre Tripet for their hard work during the photo sessions at my
club, ACBB. It went smoothly, not least because of the experience of the
judo photographer, David Finch. His unequalled library of competition
judo photographs has also made a valuable contribution to *Harai-Goshi*.

I am grateful for the permission to quote from contest judo by Saburo
Matsushita and Warwick Stepto (Foulsham 1961), and to use selected
photographs.

Typeset by Acūté, Stroud, Glos.
Printed and bound in Great Britain by Dotesios Ltd, Trowbridge, Wiltshire.

Cartoon by Pierre Roussel. Extra photographs by J.C. Bourguet.
Permission for reproduction of the cartoon by the French Judo Federation.

Contents

Foreword

The demonstration photographs present one of the major difficulties in producing good technical books for judo. It is only too easy to allow a slight dullness to creep in even where the technical points are of real interest. But no one looking at the demonstration photographs in this book can miss the dynamism in the techniques of Jean-Luc Rougé. Despite his time-consuming job as Technical Director of the French Judo Federation, it is evident that he has lost little of the vigour and precision which was so much a hallmark of his judo. Throughout the 1970s he was one of the most exciting judo competitors on the international scene, and most of his appearances in the major competitions – the Olympics, World Championships, the Europeans – and his many successes in front of his home crowd in Paris, were punctuated by *harai-goshi*.

In 1975, he won the world light heavyweight title, the first Frenchman to do so. His winning technique in the final was *harai-goshi* which demonstrates his affinity for the throw. Therefore, he was the obvious choice to write this book. Typically, he has given a stimulating analysis. Very much the realist, he has not attempted to say 'This is the way to do *harai-goshi*'. Instead, he presents the various crucial ingredients in terms of the grips, the direction of attack and the throwing, and says it is up to each individual to arrive at the correct mix for his or her own particular strengths.

It will come as no surprise to see that while he is acutely aware of the classical styles, he injects his broad competition experience into the study. He knows very clearly which techniques will work in contest, and which are more for randori or club practice. Few judoka, no matter how experienced, will read this book without learning something new.

Nicolas Soames
Masterclass Series Editor

Harai-Goshi: a Personal View

I was thirteen years old when I started judo. A friend of my father's opened a club in the small town of Gif-sur-Yvette, in the valley of Chevreuse. There was not much else to do – only football and dancing, and I was not really interested in either of those. But from the start I loved judo.

I was tall so my teacher, George Houget, taught me *harai-goshi* from an early age. I had to learn it both to the left and right – a basic lesson which made a great impression on me. It meant that I could attack on both sides with confidence, even though I was principally a right-sided fighter.

As a teenager, I was an all-action player. I was always moving and attacking, and this suits all hip techniques such as *harai-goshi*, which you can use from many different angles. I used *harai-goshi* when I won my first European title, the Espoirs, in 1967, at 85 kilos.

It again served me well when I won the European Junior Championships at 93 kilos in 1969, the year when I also won my first senior French title. I used it in conjunction with other main throws, especially *osoto-gari* and *uchi-mata*. As with many judo fighters, the technique came and went during my competitive years; at some competitions *harai-goshi* seemed to work more than anything else and, at other times, almost without reason, I turned to other techniques. However, I knew that I could always rely on it to get me out of trouble, or when I really needed something special, as in the final of the World Championships in Vienna in 1975.

I first began to realize what a powerful technique it is when I went to Japan in 1968 at the age of nineteen. My *harai-goshi* was quite strong but many of my randori opponents in the universities were puzzled by my feints and mixture of grips. This allowed me to use *harai-goshi* a lot and gave me the opportunity to study it seriously.

I was inspired, in any case, by the work of a compatriot, Guy Auffray, a *harai-goshi* specialist who won the first world medal for France, a bronze in the 1971 World Championships, in Ludwigshafen.

Fig 1   Jean-Luc Rougé celebrates after winning the world light-heavyweight title in Vienna, 1975.

I encountered many difficulties with *harai-goshi* also. As people began to get to know my techniques, they started to stop my *harai-goshi*. I realized that somehow I had to cut down the standard entry from the classical three steps to two steps and eventually one step. It was in 1972, the year before I won my first European title, that I started to develop the spin turn, which was based on a huge leap in the air. I knew it was a risky move, but I also knew that once I had launched it, it was quite difficult to stop, not least because its very action brought my opponent well off-balance. It took me some years to improve the accuracy of the movement, but eventually it became one of my strongest techniques.

By the time I arrived at the European Championships in Madrid in 1973, my repertoire was largely established. I attacked liberally with *harai-goshi* and, in the semifinal against Muzaev (Soviet Union) suddenly switched to left *ashi-guruma*, and over he went.

Observers often think I do *harai-goshi* right and left – and I do. However, generally (and particularly against bigger men) I attack right

with *harai-goshi*, but when I switch left I change to *ashi-guruma*. It works so well because there is not only a change of direction but also a different feeling in the attack: instead of sweeping my opponent's lower half, I am blocking and wheeling over my opponent's upper half. However, without my initial *harai-goshi* attacks, it would not have worked so well.

Two years later, in Vienna in 1975, I won the world light heavyweight title, the first Frenchman to do so. In the third round against the Soviet fighter Betanov, right at the end of the fight, I saw an opening for *harai-goshi*, attacked immediately, threw, and went straight down into newaza, holding him for ippon.

The final was tougher. I faced Ishibashi (Japan), but even at the start I was exhausted. Things seemed to happen automatically. I tried everything I could – *osoto-gari, uchimata, ouchi-gari* – and I defended automatically. Then, apparently out of nowhere, came my *harai-goshi*. I think I attacked with *osoto-gari* again and then the *harai-goshi* followed. It was not a classic technique, but it took Ishibashi in to the air and put him on his side for yuko, the score of the match.

I used *harai-goshi* for the remainder of my career, in France and abroad during my two other European titles (in 1977 and 1980), and for the silver and bronze I won in the World Championships in 1979. I retired in 1980. Therefore, throughout my career, *harai-goshi* proved its effectiveness. I knew it served men such as Wilhelm Ruska before me, and would remain a technique for the future also.

Harai-goshi remained such a favourite with me not only for practical reasons but because I have always thought of it as a noble technique, especially when done in the classical style. It involves the total commitment of the thrower who must forget about the danger of a counter and pit him or herself against the odds to bring off the technique which at best has all the magnificent elements of the finest spectacle. For me, this is what judo is really all about.

A History of Harai-Goshi

In the *Gokyo*, Jigoro Kano's compilation of the main judo techniques, *harai-goshi* appears in the second section – Dainikyo – as the seventh technique, after *tai-otoshi* and before *uchimata*. It has been one of the central pillars of *nage-waza*, judo's throwing techniques, since the very early days when Kano not only taught but practised it. Its development is one of the best documented among all judo techniques because it grew out of Kano's own experience.

Kano's studies at the Kito Ryu ju-jitsu school gave him a preference for throwing techniques, even though he recognized the importance of groundwork in a complete system. His tokui-waza was *uki-goshi* (floating hip), a technique which he used effectively throughout his active practising life. Film records of Kano demonstrating the throw in later life show, as could be expected, admirable style. Many of his students in the first years of judo came to him with some ju-jitsu experience and it did not take them long to discover that, in general

randori, they could avoid his *uke-goshi* by slipping over Kano's attacking hip.

Faced with this regular occurrence, Kano – a widely respected academic as well as the founder of judo – put his mind to the problem. *Harai-goshi* was the answer. As his opponents attempted to evade *uki-goshi*, Kano controlled them in mid-air, raised one leg and swept them into the air.

This story is particularly well known, not least because it is enshrined in *Nage-no-Kata*, the demonstration of throws. It comes in the second section – hip techniques – for *harai-goshi* is formally classified as *koshi-waza*. Thus the name *harai-goshi* (sweeping hip or sweeping loin in English and, in French, *hanche fauchée*) accurately describes the throw.

Harai comes from the Japanese word *harau* to sweep (to the side), and is intended to describe the basic feeling of the technique. It is supposed to be similar to *harai-tsuri-komi-ashi* or *de-ashi-barai*, even though the tech-

Fig 2(a) Saburo Matsushita throwing Akio Kaminaga in the finals of the students championships in Japan. Note the double lapel grip and the excellent upper body contact – even at the end of the throw.

(b) Once again Matsushita throws Kaminaga – in the Young Men's Championships – this time with *harai-makikomi*.

niques look very different. But *harau* also has the implication of 'brush off', as if brushing off some dust from one's jacket, which is a particularly appropriate image.

Goshi comes from *koshi* (hip). In Japanese the first sound is often hardened when it comes in the middle of a compound word, in the same way that *harai* becomes *barai* in *okuri-ashi-barai*.

A number of distinguished judoka made *harai-goshi* their principal technique, or one of two or three main throws in their repertoire. In the late 1950s and early 1960s, Saburo Matsushita was a respected exponent of the throw. When a student he won the Japanese Students Championships, throwing Akio Kaminaga (later All-Japan Champion, 1960) for ippon in the final with a superb right-handed *harai-goshi* from a double lapel grip.

During his influential days teaching at London's The Budokwai in the early 1960s, Matsushita was known as the '*Harai-Goshi* Machine'. However, as Tony Sweeney, British, international and senior instructor at The Budokwai pointed out, this was not because

he used just one technique. Matsushita was particularly known for his circular entry, stepping to one side and then spinning in, but the strength of his technique relied on his ability to vary the entry, the combinations and the grips. Therefore, while it appeared that he was throwing all the time with the same throw, he was effectively changing the circumstances considerable in order to bewilder his opponents.

Matsushita was right-handed, and was known for a regular, almost obsessive movement: before throwing, his head would flick to the left, as if he was glancing over his left shoulder, which generally presaged a *harai-goshi* of momentous proportions. There were two theories about this. The first was that, as a student of Nihon University, he was accustomed to working in a small dojo and, just before he threw, he wanted to make sure he was not going to land his opponent on another member of the club. The second was that the flick of the head was carefully co-ordinated with the basic *kuzushi*, and helped to bring uke (the opponent) on to his right foot.

Fig 3   Robert van de Walle (Belgium) throws Istvan Szeps: (Hungary) on his way to the light-heavyweight title in the Moscow Olympics 1980.

Fig 4(a) and (b)   Mrs Roger Watt wrote one of the first books on ju-jitsu to be written in England. *The Fine Art o Jujitsu* was published in 1906 and dedicated to Her Grace, the Duchess of Bedford 'with grateful affection'. She called this technique '*koshiharai*', and was clearly no mean demonstrator, although she may have been helped by her able uke, Raku Uyenishi, one of the first teachers in the west.

Though he was known mainly for *harai-goshi*, he taught a grouping of throws. In his book *Contest Judo*, written with Warwick Stepto (Foulsham, 1961), he wrote: 'If you decide to specialize in *harai-goshi* you should make *sasae-tsuri-komi-goshi* your second throw and either *osoto-gari* or *ouchi-gari* your third throw, to deal with a possible *jigotai*.' As a *harai-goshi* specialist, Matsushita was only too aware that the throw is particularly useful against an upright opponent who is not afraid to move across the mat, but the specialist must have secondary techniques to deal with more static and defensive postures.

12

Techniques

Harai-goshi is one of the most spectacular of throws in judo as can be seen in the photographs of contests down the ages, but that is not necessarily the reason for its enduring popularity. It is popular because it is a very versatile technique, one which can be executed in many directions from many starting points.

It can be done primarily as a hip technique or with more emphasis on the sweeping leg. It can be done as a direct attack or as part of a series of combinations – here, the opportunities are endless. Also, there are numerous entries and gripping options, from the sophisticated to the downright simple.

Though generally regarded as a throw for the taller men and women in judo – certainly in general club randori – the days of weight categories means that it can be effectively used by all weights, regardless of height.

Of course, *harai-goshi* has its disadvantages. It is a throw executed while standing on one leg, an inherently unbalanced position. It is also generally necessary to get in close with the hip, thus leaving tori (the attacker) open to counters from his opponent, especially *ura-nage*, the big rear throw. It can be an unnerving business when, every time you attack with *harai-goshi*, you feel the opponent waiting like a lion in bushes, ready to pounce, encircling his arm around your waist and lifting you high and backwards.

It is not, therefore, a throw for the faint-hearted or the technically ill-equipped. Careful attention has to be paid to that most basic of judo principles (but one that is so often neglected) – *kuzushi*, the breaking of the opponent's balance. If *kuzushi* is properly achieved then the throw is on. Of course, there are ways of attacking relatively safely and, as is the case throughout judo, there are times when it is necessary to settle for second best. When the chance for an upright textbook technique has been stopped it may be possible to retrieve the situation with a *makikomi* version.

At its most ideal form, *harai-goshi* demands the best principle of the Japanese budo tradition, where the attacker discards all doubt and fear of failure and, thinking only of success, throws him or herself totally into the technique. This is what characterizes so much of the best of judo. Behind it lies that state of mind – a hero's courage and purpose – which Jigoro Kano was so keen to produce through judo. It is there in the heart of *harai-goshi*.

Uki-Goshi (Fig 5)
(Sliding Hip)

Keynote
This was the *tokui-waza* (favourite technique) of Jigoro Kano, the founder of judo. It was the throw he was said to have used with singular success in the encounter with the huge Russian wrestler on board a ship and it remains an effective technique a century later.

In France we regard it as one of the best techniques to teach to beginners because even the inexperienced can control the fall of their partners. At the same time, however, both people involved can learn a lot about basic judo principles such as *kuzushi* (breaking of the balance), hip placement, personal balance and, for the person being thrown, clean break-falls with little sense of panic.

(a)   I step in, ensuring that my hip comes in at right angles, making a T-shape with my opponent. It is not *o-goshi*, when the hip comes much further through. My right hand goes around the waist and I bring my opponent's weight slightly on to his toes.

(b)   My knees bend and my hip makes contact, aided both by the pull with my left hand and, most important of all, the arm around the waist.

(c) I bend forward, rocking the weight of my opponent on to my hip. If I have not prepared for this by the slight *kuzushi* at the start, he can defend by sinking his weight and leaning backwards. At this stage, I should have absolute control. I start to raise my opponent by straightening my legs.

(d) It is then a simple matter to draw him round. As the photograph shows, I can give him good protection.

(f) This attack highlights an important point. Note that on this occasion my feet are closer together. This indicates that *harai-goshi* is now possible, because it is easy for me to transfer all my weight on to one foot in order to reap with the other. When my feet are wide apart, the change to *harai-goshi* is more difficult.

(e) The fall is clean.

(a)   In the kata, *harai-goshi* is demonstrated on the move, with my opponent coming forward, pushing slightly as if in attack.

(b)   I retreat, drawing him forwards with my left hand on the sleeve, and slipping my right hand under his arm, placing it on the shoulder blade. My left foot comes quite far round. It will take all my opponent's weight and so must be accurately placed in relation to the drawing of his body-weight forward.

Harai-Goshi – Nage-No-Kata-Style (Fig 6) (Sweeping Hip)

Keynote
This is the form of *harai-goshi* used in *Nage-No-Kata* and, as can be seen from the grips, it is very close to *uki-goshi*.

(c)   This is the crucial position. At this point, I must have very good upper body contact – any gaps will ruin the technique. Once this ideal contact is obtained, the rest of my body will follow in the technique. In this photograph it can be seen that although my opponent is not bent over in an exaggerated manner, he is leaning slightly on his right leg. It is now easy for me to sweep.

Note   This position is important for the basic study of upper body contact and control of uke.

(d) I make an exaggerated movement with my sweeping leg, bringing it high, pointing my toes. While rarely possible in randori or contest, it helps to provide a detailed awareness of the sweeping action, develops power, and trains my general balance on my standing leg. Observe, also, how my standing leg is bent. If it is stiff at this juncture, the whole technique will be stiff, and I will be more prone to overbalancing.

(e) As I sweep, the body acts like a see-saw, an image which emphasizes the need for continued upper body contact. The feeling must be of both bodies glued together, but I am in command.

(f) This is aided by my right arm on my opponent's shoulder blade as can be clearly seen. As I throw, I do not lose my balance and fall on top of him, but I put him on the spot where I would naturally fall were I to topple. The direction of the throw is an important aspect.

(g) In this demonstration, I give my opponent support for the fall.

Note The throwing action for this form of *harai-goshi* involves an equal amount of hip and leg attack.

Stepping Patterns

Keynote
There are so many variations in stepping patterns for *harai-goshi* that it is best to indicate the two extremes and the general principles involved. There are many factors to be taken into account, varying from the height and action of the opponent to his or her response and the direction of the throw.

Harai-Goshi: Lateral (Fig 7)

Keynote
I call this 'lateral' because the whole feeling of the throw is to one side, very different to the classical, *Nage-No-Kata* style. It is basically quite simple, and useful for contest because the movement range is relatively small. It is, therefore, quite fast, but all details must be precise for it to work well.

It is best used against an opponent who may be the same height or slightly smaller, and has a tendency to lean back in defence.

(a) The first step, made with the left foot, is very important. Standing in *hon-shizentai* (normal face to face, right hand grips), I step sharply to my left and slightly backwards, moving only my left foot. My foot must be very accurately placed – note that it is slightly turned.

At exactly the same time my arms take my opponent's off-balance, putting all his weight on to his right foot. The breaking of balance is done by the right arm, gripping the lapel, driving across like a punch, yet allowing my right elbow to slip under his armpit. This is easier if I am slightly smaller than my opponent. My left hand pulls strongly too. All these actions take place simultaneously in one firm but aggressive motion.

At this stage, my opponent is not quite sure what I am attacking with. He cannot see my turned-left foot, and feels that the attack may be *harai-goshi* or even *osoto-gari* but, in any case, he should not be in a position to defend against either. Note how most of his weight is on his right foot.

(b) It is then a simple matter to step through the gap, so to speak, and get into sweeping position. This must be done smoothly, but alertly, as I cannot hold my opponent in such a favourable position for more than a split second.

A number of points must be made about the throw. I have tucked my right elbow well under his left armpit. This, in conjunction with my sleeve grip, gives me good control of the upper body. However, I am not looking for a big, classical semicircular throwing motion. I want to throw my partner to my right side. With that upper body control, I can rotate my partner where he stands, emphasizing once again what a quick throw this is.

The main impetus for the throw comes from the attacking leg, which acts more in a reaping manner than truly sweeping. The lateral version of *harai-goshi* should feel to the opponent like a short, sharp shock.

Harai-Goshi: Semicircular (Fig 8)

Keynote

This is best used against a slightly taller and heavier opponent. Tori must make a large movement quickly, but he can also bring his hip into play, generating considerable power.

(a) My opponent is pushing forward slightly and, in a response similar to the *harai-goshi* in *Nage-no-Kata*, I turn, spinning on the spot. This is the principle.

I am holding traditional sleeve/lapel grip, and I need to 'open up' my opponent slightly as he pushes forward in order to take control of his balance and achieve good body position. Ideally, I want to slip my right arm under his armpit. In fact, as the photograph shows, I make a complete 180° turn – most of the success of the throw depends on that accurate placing of my left leg. The deeper it goes in between my partner's legs, the easier he will be to throw. In competition or even strong randori, this is quite difficult to achieve, but spectacular when it does happen.

(b) I am now in a position to bring the attacking leg into play. I can afford to sweep deeply – in the semicircular version most of the sweeping action actually comes from the hips.

Notice that the direction of the throw is considerably different to the lateral version.

Conclusion

The lateral and semicircular versions of *harai-goshi* represent the opposite poles of opportunity. There are many divisions in between but at first it is necessary to be totally clear about the details and the implications of these two.

19

Hip Placements

I have already mentioned that *harai-goshi* attacks vary according to the amount of emphasis placed on the hip or sweeping leg for the throwing action. In fact, the placing of the hip is one of the central aspects of the throw, and a clear understanding of the function in every variation is crucial. Here are two examples of the extremes.

Minimum Hip (Fig 9)

Keynote

It is often difficult to get one's hip across into the conventional *harai-goshi* position when faced with a strong, upright but pushing defence. However, it is still possible to use the throw.

(a)   Holding a sleeve and high collar grip, I use a standard entry but because of the strong defence, I cannot get in as deep as I would like, but have managed to break my opponent's balance slightly. The important element here is the gripping. Although I have not gained shoulder contact, I 'fix' the upper body control so that there is no movement or flexing.

(b)   I lean away, bringing him with me, ensuring all the while that from thigh to my shoulder control the contact remainst the same. This is partly achieved by remaining quite relaxed on my standing leg – notice how I have bent a little deeper.

(c)   Now I can sweep my opponent off his feet.

Maximum Hip (Fig 11)

Keynote
This is useful against an opponent who is noticeably bent over in a defensive but weak posture.

The 'Normal' Position (Fig 10)

Fig 10 Right in the centre of the two extremes is what one can term the 'normal' hip placement.

(a) I use the same sleeve/high collar grip and the same entry, although I lead with the hip. I am virtually in position for *koshi-guruma*, but he threatens to slip off my hip. Once again, it is important that I 'fix' my gripping control from the shoulders right down to my hip.

(b) I start to sweep. Notice how, as I have bent forward to take my partner off-balance, I have been careful not to let him create a gap. If anything I have tightened the control. My hip is well through, yet it is still the fulcrum for the see-saw action.

(c) My sweeping action finishes the throw.

21

Special Stepping Patterns and Entries

The purpose of the following techniques is to put my opponent in the position which makes him vulnerable to *harai-goshi*, which generally means bringing his weight on to his right foot.

Lateral Entry 1 (Fig 12)

Keynote
The basic purpose here is to fix uke on his right leg, and to get inside his defending arms using his own reaction. This is a particular favourite of mine because at the beginning it can feel to uke like *ouchi-gari*. This encourages him to bring his weight forward, on to his right foot, which is where I want it.

(a)   I do not move my left leg.

(b)   I bring my right foot across. It is very important to place my right foot in the correct position, slightly turned away. It is not a very beautiful position, but I can assure you it is effective. At this juncture, my opponent's weight will be slightly on his right leg.

(c)   My arms perform a small lifting action. As my left leg shoots backwards and I turn my body round, I go up a little with him, harmonizing with his movement. It is a small detail but makes all the difference to the smooth quality of the attacking action.

(d) However, as soon as my left leg hits the mat, I pull down firmly with both arms, fixing my opponent's body to mine. I am now in a strong position to sweep him off his feet . . .

(e) and (f) . . . which I duly do.

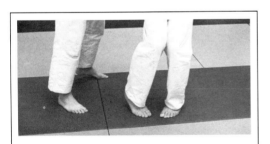

(g) and (h) A close-up of my feet shows the action clearly.

Lateral Entry 2 (Fig 13)

Keynote
This is based on a movement pattern in harmony with my opponent. I do little more than just follow, and then step in at the appropriate moment. Although this is a clear *harai-goshi*, sometimes the actual throw can be quite close to *osoto-gari*.

(a)   Generally, I start the action. I take a small step backwards, bringing my opponent with me.

(b)   He reacts by pulling back and I follow. He now begins to worry about *osoto-gari* and thinks of taking his right leg back out of reach. This works to my advantage.

(c)   I pivot on my left foot – note the change of direction which indicates that *harai-goshi* is coming – and I step across. That small adjustment of my left foot has altered the whole direction of the ensuing throw. If my opponent is tall, I pull him down; if he is small, I pull him up.

(d)   Now I fix my opponent's body to mine – and sweep him into the air. My sweeping leg works hard here; the hip does little. Note the direction of the throw.

(e)   This often proves a very clean ippon. I used this quite often in my contest career because my opponents were worried about *osoto-gari* and left themselves open for *harai-goshi*.

The Waves (Fig 14)

Keynote

This is a curious technique – and more suited to randori than competition – although I saw Isamu Sonoda use something similar in Japan. It is dangerous in contest to make such a large movement, but practising this in randori helps you to develop a bold and smooth movement pattern.

(a) I hold my opponent lightly. I step away, still quite light in the arms but hanging my body-weight slightly on him.

The general principle is to go far away, provoking a break of balance and then move swiftly back into attacking range to reap the benefit. This technique is like the powerful ebb and flow of the waves upon the shore.

Note The secret – and the fun – of this technique is in the dynamism of the whole action, as demonstrated in Fig 14(c).

(c) I step with my right foot, hanging my weight even more on my opponent. This is the turning point of the throw – I am now ready to go back into the attack.

(b) Now I step away firmly, bringing him on to his right foot.

(d) and (e) I retreat quickly and the combination of the surprise and the speed takes my opponent right off his feet.

Spinning Entry (Fig 15)

Keynote

In French, this is called *cloche pied,* and it is one of my special favourites. It is an explosive technique and can be used in a static position. It comes as a surprise because there is no preparatory step. I started it in 1972 and I used it many times during my career. In the final of the 1980 European Championships, I threw Dietmar Lorenz of East Germany with it for ippon in the first minute.

I must be strong enough to keep a bit of distance between myself and my opponent because I need the space in which to turn, but having pushed (if necessary) to create the distance, I must then relax the arms and let them go soft in order to turn.

(a) I start the spin. The idea is to wind up like a spring. The right knee comes up in order to develop a good torque, starting from the right foot as it comes across.

(b) and (c) This is all about dynamism. The slightest hesitation or doubt will stop this technique even getting off the ground.

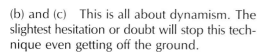

(d) When my left leg hits the tatami and the turn is complete, I must strengthen my grip, clamping my partner to me. Only then am I ready to sweep.

(e) and (f)   The throw should feel all part of the same action; there should be no break in the whole movement.

Sometimes, against a nervous, jerky opponent, it is possible just to touch the calf as I have done here. This provokes a reaction against the threat of *ouchi-gari*, which opens him up for the *cloche pied* entry.

Training – Spinning Entry (Fig 16)

Fig 16 exaggerates the movement a little for training purposes.

(a)   I sink a little to gather momentum for the spring up.

(b)   As I come up, my foot starts to come across.

(c)   Notice how high I have brought my knee though the toes are leading. I come right off the ground at the height of the spin. As soon as I touch the mat again, I pull firmly.

(d)   In training, I take my sweeping foot as far away as possible to generate maximum power.

Circling Entry (Fig 17)
(Also Traditionally Known as Spin Entry)

Keynote

When I started judo, this kind of large, free movement was often seen, but as competitive judo became stronger and more defensive it became more difficult to do, as strong gripping can kill it dead. Nevertheless, it is worthwile spending some time working on this entry in randori because it helps to develop bold and smooth general movement and also a good style.

(a) My stance and initial movement seem like a left-hand attack to my opponent. He begins to lean to his right as a counter-balance, which is exactly the reaction I am seeking.

Notice my grip. My left hand has taken the cloth by the armpit, over my opponent's right arm, although a normal sleeve grip will do. My right hand has taken an inside high collar grip. This is a grip I used a lot because I found it offered both versatility and control.

(b) My arms are quite soft as I prepare for the turn. If they are stiff, I cannot move quickly, and speed of entry is very important here. I step across boldly.

(c) I gain maximum impetus by jumping into the turn — my right leg makes a considerable swing.

28

(d)   In full flight, but working like a spinning top.

(e)   As soon as I hit the ground and I achieve a stable base, my arms pull in tight. Considerable accuracy is required at this point for the throw to be effective: Firstly, my body position must be correct. A wild entry which places me too far to the left or right, or unbalances me on my left foot, is useless. Secondly, my right hand employs a special action – called 'Geesink' style in Europe and 'Tenri' style in Japan. The right wrist bends upwards and exerts a strong pressure against the left side of my opponent's jaw or upper neck. Thirdly, my left hand pulls down, my left elbow trapping his arm.

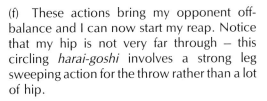

(f)   These actions bring my opponent off-balance and I can now start my reap. Notice that my hip is not very far through – this circling *harai-goshi* involves a strong leg sweeping action for the throw rather than a lot of hip.

(g)   My spinning impetus continues and as I throw I turn well to my left.

Grips

A variety of grips can be used for *harai-goshi* and its attendant throws. In France, we try not to teach a particular grip for a particular throw. We say that here is a throw and its variations, and here are various grips that can be used with them. It is like a *salade mixte* – everyone can choose the ingredients to suit themselves, depending on their different physiques and their body movements. If the choice is a good one, the throw will work; if not, it is necessary to look again. This encourages a lively, alert look at judo and its techniques, rather than simply following textbook patterns.

Traditional Kumi-Kata (Fig 18)

Keynote
This is the standard grip used by many *harai-goshi* specialists.

(a) The left hand takes a sleeve grip, controlling the elbow. The right hand takes a high collar grip which controls the head. Notice the taut line of the back of the jacket – I am not just resting my arm on my opponent's shoulder but controlling all the time.

(b) As I turn, the pull is parallel to the ground. My left arm pulls out and wide, with my elbow kept high. My right forearm controls the head. The effect is to put my opponent on to his right leg.

Left-Hand Down Grip (Fig 19)

Keynote
I actually prefer this variation on the traditional action.

Fig 19 My right hand works in much the same manner, but my left hand pulls my partner's hand down to my side, capturing it. This means that when I turn my body, my partner is obliged to come with me.

Geesink Style/Tenri Style (Fig 20)

Keynote
This variation is called 'Geesink style' in Europe and 'Tenri style' in Japan. Anton Geesink, the 1964 Olympic champion from the Netherlands, introduced it to Europe. It was developed in the post-war period by Matsumoto, one of the leading competitors and All-Japan champion in the post-war period. It is particularly useful for taller fighters.

Fig 20   It concerns just the right hand and involves this distinctive bending of the wrist against the left side of the opponent's face. It controls the head and forces the opponent over to the right. I use this variation when I

cannot get the undergrip which I actually prefer. However, I can use it in conjunction with my favoured left-hand grip – the cloth at the armpit.

My Favourite Grip (Fig 21)

Keynote
This was my particular favourite. I found that with this grip I could disturb the balance of my opponent, and it was generally relatively easy to get. Only when my opponents knew me very well and set out to actively stop me obtaining it did I change to other grips. It is also useful against small judogi which prevents a good grip on the sleeve.

Note   When I first went to Japan to train, many randori opponents thought I was going to attack left because my right arm was lifted up. They were surprised when I attacked right. It was with a form of this grip that Guy Auffray, a *harai-goshi* specialist, won the first bronze medal for France in the 1971 World Championships in Ludwigshafen.

(a) The principle is one of basic levers. A right hand tilt comes from raising the left elbow and bearing down on the right arm.

(b) My right arm uses a 'Geesink' wrist; my left arm bears down on the opponent's arm. It is all in the elbows.

31

Turning Against the Defending Arm 1 (Fig 22)

Keynote

This is a very basic and often-encountered problem in judo and affects many throws, not just *harai-goshi*.

(a)   My opponent defends with a strong left arm pushing into my chest, preventing me making my turn. I take the over grip with my right hand and pull myself in tight.

(b)   Having taken my sleeve grip, I bring my right arm sharply down on his elbow and bring the arm across. When the blow is accurate, it just bends.

(c)   Now I can come across for *harai-goshi*.

Turning Against the Defending Arm 2 (Fig 23)

Keynote
This is done at more of a distance and is useful if your opponent is very strong and prevents you getting close. Instead of aiming at the elbow, you aim at the wrist.

(a) Once again I take the over grip and lean away slightly.

(b) Now I attack my opponent's wrist with my elbow, leaning against it.

(c) I come in a bit like a *yama-arashi* action, turning into the space between us.

(d) My opponent's defence has been totally negated – note his bent left arm – and I can break his balance.

(e) Now I have good control and I can sweep and turn.

Back Grip 1 (Fig 24)

Keynote

The back grip is very strong for *harai-goshi* because it offers control as well as freedom to move. A lot of these back grips are used by Russian-style fighters, those who have good balance once they are in close to an opponent.

(a) It is particularly easy to get a back grip against a left-handed opponent. Notice how I have started to negate his defending left arm, sliding it off my chest with a shrug of my shoulder as I take the grip.

(b) Once I have the grip I can pull him in and turn.

Back Grip 2 (Fig 25)

Keynote

This can be effectively used by much taller fighters, or those with long arms. It often works best when the attack with the arm comes out of a confusion of movement with arms and feet. Just to reach over from a solid base invites a pick-up counter.

(a) The basic action. Pulling in strongly with the left hand, I reach over for the cloth.

(b) Grasping firmly, I turn in for *harai-goshi*. Note the turn of my upper body and head.

Belt Grip 1 (Fig 26)

Keynote

This illustrates the belt grip, but also the general feeling of an attack using this kind of grip from a flurry of action. *See* Khouboulouri throw with this technique on page 88.

(a)–(h) It can be even more effective if I manage to take hold of the belt. This is a real power technique, judo wrestling-style. Notice how I stand left at the start, pull away sharply, and then make my attack for the belt. There is a lot of hip action in the throw.

Belt Grip 2 (Fig 27)

Keynote
A more unusual belt grip variation, and one that can be a surprise. Remember, the belt can only be held while making an attack or for the duration of three seconds.

(a) I reach down for the belt at the front with my right hand.

(b)–(f) I step in and throw, using a lot of hip action to make the throw.

The Hug (Fig 28)

Keynote
This is just a trick, but one that can work from time to time.

(a)   We stand face to face, a little reluctant to actually take grip.

(b)   As my opponent raises his hands hesitantly, I dart into action, slapping his hands down a little.

(c)   I attack between his hands.

(d)   My arms encircle him in a hugging motion.

(e)   Now I can throw.

(a)   My opponent is coming forward but it is difficult to grip with my right hand.

Harai-Makikomi 1 (Fig 29) (Sweeping Winding Throw)

Keynote

Makikomi is often seen in competition, though some people think it is not particularly good style. However, it is certainly effective and sometimes, when the defence is strong, the situation simply calls for it.

(b)   I spin on my right foot, reaching over with my right hand.

(c)–(f)   I continue the rotation all the way down to the ground. Notice the pointed foot in Fig 25(e). This ensures good rotational action.

Fig 30   Robert van de Walle, inflamed by his defeat at the hands of Marc Meiling in the semifinal of the light-heavyweight category of the Seoul Olympics stormed back through the repêchage, throwing the 1984 Olympic silver medallist Robert Berland (USA) with this powerful *harai-makikomi*.

(f)   (g)

Harai-Makikomi 2 (Fig 31)

Keynote
This was the way I tended to use *harai-makikomi*.

(a) I attacked with *harai-goshi*. My opponent knew it was coming and managed to get all his weight on his left leg.

(b) My right shoulder is being pulled backwards. I let go with my right arm and lean forward. Now I am in a position to continue the turn, but I continue to trap his leg with my foot.

(c) I grab hold of his sleeve and turn (see Fig 26(j)). Note that I have hopped backwards slightly with my left leg to get in a bit tighter.

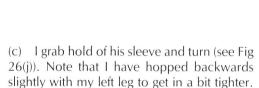

(d)–(h) The feeling of this strong rotational action is of doing a rolling breakfall. This ensures that my opponent is taken well on to his back and I end up in total control.

(e)

(f)

(g)

(h)

(i)   A detail of the hands.

41

Eri Harai-Goshi (Fig 32)
(Lapel Harai-Goshi)
Keynote

This is a useful technique to break up a strong defensive grip. It is especially appropriate for a smaller man against a larger opponent.

(a)   I hold with both hands on one side, the left hand taking the sleeve, the right the lapel. I pull up high to make room for my hip.

(b)–(e)   I tuck in well with my hip and throw – using a lot of hip action.

Lapel Grip Only (Fig 33)

Keynote

Often at the top contest level it can be difficult to get ideal grips. Sometimes it is necessary to make the best of a bad deal.

(a)   I take the under grip. Notice how I have taken hold with my left hand. I must be careful not to put on an armlock, and under relatively recent rules, if I go down to the ground using this grip I can be penalized.

(b)   I make a lateral entry, stepping across with my right foot, and tucking my left in behind as deep between my opponent's legs as I can.

(c)   I must make as deep an entry as possible because I want to prevent my opponent from getting his hand down on the mat.

(d) and (e)   The ideal situation. It does not often happen as conclusively as this, but it can be enough to unsettle an opponent and open him up for something else.

43

Ashi-Guruma (Fig 34)
(Foot Wheel)

Keynote

This may not be *harai-goshi* but it is an important addition to a *harai-goshi* armoury because it can be used effectively against an opponent with an acute right-handed stance and a strong defensive attitude.

When done at speed it often looks very like *harai-goshi* but the feeling is very different. Traditionally it is described as a wheeling action, with the attacking leg just blocking (not sweeping as in *harai-goshi*) and the hands wheeling the opponent over on to his back. But to me the feeling is closer to drawing a bucket of water from a well – with a vigorous, smooth turning motion, you pull the opponent off the ground and on to his back.

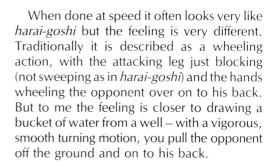

(a) My opponent adopts an acute stance protecting his left leg and defending with his arms. I grip both lapels, my left hand taking the under grip. (This grip will play a crucial role in unbalancing my partner by raising his elbow.) My right hand takes the over grip. I raise my knee in preparation.

(b) I flick my leg across, trapping his leg just above the knee. It just blocks, but maintains pressure.

(c) Now, this is all about rotation. There is still quite a distance between myself and my opponent – I need space to turn. As I turn, note how my left foot turns too, but maintains the pressure all the time. Therefore, I have control of my opponent from the top right down to the furthest extremity. This is important. It can be difficult at the start to feel this strict and tight control, and yet still be relaxed enough to make a good turn on the right foot. The danger is that you freeze altogether.

(d) The grips come forcefully into play now. My left arm forces the elbow across and my right pulls down, trapping the left hand (otherwise an opponent can put his hand out and prevent the throw).

Ashi-Guruma (Fig 35)

Keynote
This is one opening for *ashi-guruma*.

(a) My opponent is defending against right *harai-goshi* and my right-hand collar grip.

(b) I force his head up with the 'Geesink' wrist, but he still pushes against it.

(c) Suddenly I switch to left *ashi-guruma*, helped by the push of his own head.

(e) Note my bent right leg as I continue the turn, and the pointed toes of my left foot.

(f) I wheel him over.

Hane-Goshi (Fig 36) (Spring Hip)

Keynote

Hane-goshi is often mentioned in the same breath as *harai-goshi* though it is rarely seen in international competition now, mainly because it is a difficult throw to bring off in a defensive environment.

However, there is one form of *hane-goshi* that I believe is possible. I include it in this book partly because it can work in conjunction with *harai-goshi*. The opponent is expecting *harai-goshi* but, instead of attacking with a sweeping action, one attacks in the front with a lifting/pushing action. I have found it particularly useful against left-handed fighters because I can get the belt grip easily.

I met Angelo Parisi, the 1980 Olympic champion, in the semifinal of the Tournoi de Paris in 1978. I do not remember deciding to do this *hane-goshi*, I just attacked with it. Parisi seemed to explode into the air and went flying across the mat as if he was the star villain in one of those Chinese martial arts films. Ooh la la. It was the best ippon of my life.

(a)   A static start. I prepare the grips – an armpit grip with the left hand and a back grip with the right.

(b)   I step in, turning my left foot well in the direction of the throw. It may look awkward, but it is possible. I must bend my knee considerably.

(c)   The break of balance here must be strong, almost as if I was about to do *tomoe-nage*.

(d) I step across at great speed. Note the angle of our bodies – they must be both leaning at the same angle.

(f) I do not turn to the left to throw, but just rotate my opponent's body on the spot.

(e) As my leg connects, I must obtain good upper body control and contact. Once again, it is a see-saw feeling with the leg lifting and the arms pulling down as my head goes down.

(g) and (h) I place him down by my side – we call this a 'percussion' technique. It is very fast, explosive and sudden.

Note It is worth *harai-goshi* specialists having a go at this. Most of the work done will aid the general *harai-goshi* practice in any case.

Combinations

Combinations are about reactions. One person attacks and the other reacts in a particular fashion, and just exactly what they do often says a lot about the person.

The majority of people in judo, and especially in top competition, just react instinctively to a strong attack. They do not respond in a thinking, creative, varied way. They do the same thing every time. This kind of competitor is a computer. He or she has been trained to react in one way, and will tend to repeat the pattern if a similar attack is mounted, because in both randori and competition, things can happen so fast that there is normally no time to think. The reaction may be a simple block, or it may take the more creative form of a counter-attack, especially if the counter-attacker knows the *tokui-waza* of the opponent and can prepare for it.

The problem is that a capable opponent can read the reaction and, by thinking a further step ahead, can utilize that reaction to throw. To be predictable is to be vulnerable.

This is what combinations are based upon: predictable reactions. You attack, provoke a reaction, and deal with it. This is why, incidentally, beginners are very often difficult to throw with combinations – they just have not been programmed with the expected reactions. This is one example of why judo has to be varied according to the opponent you are facing.

Another factor which has to be taken into account is the size of the opponent. Someone who is smaller and lighter than you is likely to have a faster reaction time, and be living on his or her nerves. Therefore, it is necessary to use techniques which just require a feint rather than a full-blooded attack. When dealing with larger, slower opponents, however, it may be necessary to launch a strong, committed first attack in order to really convince them that something is truly happening. Then you still may have to wait for them to get into the correct position before attacking with the second barrel of the gun.

Combinations are one of the most fascinating and creative aspects of judo. I used them

Fig 37   A typical *osoto-gake/harai-goshi* mixed attack so often seen in contest. Here, Bernard Tchoullyan attacks Andrade (Portugal) at the 1980 Moscow Olympics. Tchoullyan hooks in, but his left foot shows he is intending to throw with *harai-goshi* rather than *osoto-gake*.

(b)   Tchoullyan's right arm has come past Andrade's head but, with the elbow lifted will, he can continue to exert an effective lift-pull action.

(c)   A fraction more pull and twist from the Frenchman takes Andrade off his feet.

(d)   Finally, the throw succeeds.

extensively in both competition and randori, not least because my techniques – particularly *harai-goshi* and *osoto-gari* – were not only linked to each other with combination options, but also part of a basic blueprint for my whole attacking pattern. If I attacked with *harai-goshi* to the front and it did not work, I would watch my opponent's reaction and then un-leash either *osoto-gari*, *kouchi-gari* or *ouchi-gari* according to what he did.

Of course, I used other combinations as well, and also started with *osoto-gari* and then looked for my opponent's reaction. Sometimes my attack was just a feint – in French we call it *confusion* – sometimes it was a true attack/combination, which we call *enchainement*.

A Basic Combination Blueprint (Fig 38)

Keynote

This is one example of a combination pattern. It may be suitable for others but each person must make their own or adapt it to suit the favoured techniques. It is all based on a strong feint for *harai-goshi*, not a real *harai-goshi* attack.

If he tries to pull me back towards his left back corner, my answer is *ouchi-gari* (Fig 38(c)). If he tries to pull me directly back, my answer is *kouchi-gari* (Fig 38(b)). If he tries to pull me towards his back right corner, the answer is *osoto-gari* (Fig 38(e)). And if he doesn't react at all – well, I throw him with *harai-goshi* (Fig 38(d)). *Simple, n'est-ce pas?*

Sasae-Tsuri-Komi-Ashi into Harai-Goshi (Fig 39) (Propping, Drawing, Pulling Leg into Sweeping Hip)

Keynote
This is very possible in contest if uke is provoked into making a heavy avoidance.

(a) Holding the sleeve and high collar, I make a stab at my opponent's foot which he simply avoids.

(b) But my pull is sufficiently strong to bring him forward on to his right foot.

(c) This is a detail, taken from another sequence, but it shows my next movement — stepping away with my left foot to create space for my *harai-goshi* attack.

(d) Now I can move in for *harai-goshi* . . .

(e) . . . and throw.

Ouchi-Gari into Harai-Goshi (Fig 40) (Major Inner Reap into Sweeping Throw)

Keynote

This is a full combination because it involves a true break of balance of the opponent – a back/forwards routine. It does not happen very often in contest because it generally involves a big movement (in French we call it *deplacement*) from my opponent, and opponents are not often so relaxed. Nevertheless, it is very good educational movement when learning *harai-goshi*, because it provokes just the right reaction of a superb throw. And sometimes it can happen in competition!

(a)   I think *harai-goshi* on my first step.

(b)–(d)   But I attack sufficiently strongly with *ouchi-gari* to surprise my opponent who has to step off it and away. It may be necessary to wait at this point for him to get his left foot to the mat.

Contest Version

(e)   Then I must attack positively with *harai-goshi*, bringing my left leg round into position (between my partner's legs) in a smart and efficient manner.

When this sequence does happen in competition, this is generally the form it takes.

(f) and (g)   Then I throw – turning well to my left.

(a)–(c)   I have one of those jumpy opponents who reacts to every twitch I make, so I just touch his calf as if signalling an *ouchi-gari*. He over-reacts. I have anticipated this and I am already moving into the technique.

Note   The use of combinations varies considerably against different opponents. Some are so slow you have to wait for them to react, and some are so fast you actually have to anticipate. Get it wrong, and nothing happens. Get it right, and it can be spectacular.

Kouchi-Gari to Harai-Goshi (Fig 41) (Minor Inner Reap to Sweeping Hip)

Keynote
This is much the same idea, except on the other side.

(a)   I attack with *kouchi-gari*.

(b)   He steps off and I get in position – my left foot once again going accurately between his feet.

(c) and (d)   A smooth throw, with not so much rotation necessary. Note the difference of throwing direction from the *ouchi-gari/ harai-goshi* combination.

Osoto-Gari into Harai-Goshi (Fig 42) (Major Outer Reap into Sweeping Hip)

Keynote

This is one of the classic combinations and basically works on the same principle as the *ashi-guruma* (direct attack).

(a)   I attack with *osoto-gari*.

(b)   I hook my opponent's leg but he resists strongly by pushing forwards.

(c)   I turn on my own spot, trying to keep as much contact with my partner as possible. This is not always easy.

(d)   I throw, turning markedly to my left.

Harai-Goshi into Sukui-Nage (Fig 43)
(Sweeping Hip into Scooping Throw)

Keynote

Sukui-nage is an old judo technique. It is found in *Ju-no-Kata,* more or less in the form I demonstrate here. This is also basically a feint combination.

(a)   My initial attack is the circling entry for *harai-goshi*. My opponent starts to lean back slightly to his right.

(b)   I prepare to take an extra little jump on my left foot to bring me a little closer to the left side of my opponent.

(c)   I am now in close and starting to pull in tight with my left hand.

(d)   My right foot reaches out behind him, aiming for his far foot. At the same time, my right hand snakes through the tangle of arms in front. This is easier than it sounds.

(e) My right hand grips his thigh to pull him in even closer.

(f) I want to make my opponent sit on my thigh, because then I will know that I have perfect control and he cannot defend against the throw. I do not want any gaps at all.

(g) I can then bring him right off the ground with a small movement of my hips as I take him backwards.

(h) It is possible to gain ippon with this.

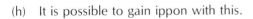

Osoto-Gari into Harai-Makikomi (Fig 44)
(Major Outer Reap into
Sweeping Winding Throw)

Keynote
Here I am facing a smaller opponent, and my natural reaction is to switch to *makikomi*, as it is much more difficult to maintain a usable grip with the right hand.

(a) and (b)   I attack with *osoto-gari* and meet with stiff defence.

(c)   As I turn and change direction, I take up my *makikomi* position. I am looking down to the spot where I want to throw my opponent.

(d)   I have contact right along the side of my body, down to my ankle.

(e)   I have turned my head well, which is the mark of all *harai-makikomi* throws.

(f)   A clean ippon – and hard.

Harai-Goshi into Kani-Basami (Fig 45) (Sweeping Hip into Crab Pinch)

Keynote

This is classed as a highly dangerous technique, but I firmly believe it is very important to judo. It is one of the main techniques which prevents a very negative side-on stance that is so common in judo. It is regarded as dangerous because uke's knees – and ankles – are sometimes injured when this throw is attempted. But uke is only injured if he tries to take

inappropriate avoidance action – and attempts to twist out of the throw. If he does not try to twist, and makes a clean breakfall, there is no danger. It is a pity, therefore, for tori to be stopped from using a valid technique because of uke's own stupidity.

I used it in my career with success against some strong opponents, including Nobuyuki Sato, David Starbrook and Jean-Paul Coche. They were all thrown, and none were injured. It is useful when the opponent is side-on, and also when he is preparing to counter-attack *harai-goshi* with *ura-nage* as is demonstrated here.

As this book was going to press, the International Judo Federation were discussing banning kani-basami from competition. However, this technique is still part of judo history, and I include it - if only for personal interest.

(a) I attack as if for *harai-goshi*, but I am standing to one side. I am holding a sleeve and have a high collar grip.

(b) I let go of the sleeve grip.

(c) I reach out to the ground with my left hand, and at the same time move my legs into position. I pull my opponent down a little so that he will respond by pulling back strongly, which he will continue to do especially if he had been thinking of *uranage*.

(d)   I want my right leg to be around waist high, and my left leg to be behind my opponent's knees, which works well for a long-legged person like me. I keep a good grip with my right hand. Now I am in the ideal position to throw.

(e)   The finish of the throw.

(f)   I continue to scissor with my legs to put him squarely on his back.

From the Other Side

(g) and (h)   The last section of the throw seen from the other side.

Counters and Defences

The versatility of *harai-goshi*, and the general applicability of the basic action, makes it an admirable counter weapon. It takes time, of course, to absorb the natural flowing movement so deeply that it is second nature. Only then is it possible to control or check an attack and have the confidence and ability to immediately launch a counter-attack.

As I pointed out in the combinations section, one of the main weaknesses of many judo fighters, even at a high level, is predictability when under attack. This is the foundation of combinations.

One of my special practices when I was training for competition was to ensure that I never made the same defence to an attack. Instead of reacting instinctively, I tried to respond. Even during the intensity of competition I would remember my responses to attacks. If I evaded the first attack, I blocked the second; if I moved to the left on the third attack, I moved to the right on the fourth. The movements had to be appropriate as, of course, the first objective was not to be thrown. I started work on this during ordinary randori

sessions and maintained it during my contest career. I know it paid off because my opponents said that I was a very unpredictable fighter. It is a skill worth developing.

In this chapter I have concentrated on *harai-goshi* as a counter, rather than the counters to *harai-goshi*. And it is true that *harai-goshi* is a throw which can be easily countered when not executed correctly. The counters vary but in the main they are along the basic theme of *uranage* or *ushiro-goshi*, or pick-ups of various kinds. One of the basic problems with *harai-goshi* is that tori has to go right across the path of uke and gain close contact, which is always a risky manoeuvre.

Part of a *harai-goshi* study is to take note of these counters when they occur, and analyse the reason, be it incorrect *kuzushi*, incorrect body position, slow speed of entry, inappropriate gripping or whatever. Only when this is done can the *harai-goshi* specialist really attack with confidence; a tentative attack is inviting a counter right from the start.

The theme of this chapter, however, is that attack is the best form of defence.

A Strong Defence Countered by Harai-Goshi (Fig 46)

Keynote

My opponent has achieved the dominant right-hand grip and may be waiting to launch a *harai-goshi*, but a sudden burst of accurate action can unsettle even the strongest defence.

(a)   My head is being pulled down by the high collar grip.

(b)   I relax slightly, push up the dominant arm and duck under it. As I do so, I bend my knees but maintain my grip.

(c)   As I regain my posture, I readjust so that I can do my spinning entry. Boldness is the key in this situation; my opponent, being stiff, will probably be slower to react.

(d) and (e)   I can now execute *harai-goshi*.

Osoto-Gari Countered by Harai-Goshi (Fig 47)

Keynote

I see this as much as a combination as a counter. My opponent's attack with *osoto-gari* really just starts my *harai-goshi* movement.

(a) The most important point here is the most obvious: don't be thrown by the *osoto-gari*.

(b) As he attacks, I bring my weight forward on my left foot.

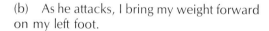

(c) This stops his attack and makes him feel vulnerable.

(d) and (e)   He starts to retreat, but I maintain the contact with the upper body.

(f)   To be able to turn I must relax my body while still maintaining control of my opponent with my arms. This is quite a skilful business because if I relax too much, he will simply throw me with *osoto-gari*, or even *harai-goshi*.

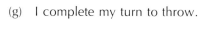

(g)   I complete my turn to throw.

Note   I found this counter effective because my *osoto-gari* is as strong as my *harai-goshi*, and I am acutely aware of the nuances of balance and control in such an interlocked situation.

Harai-Goshi Countered by Harai-Goshi (Fig 48)

Keynote

This is more of educational value than real interest for the competition environment, although it is worth trying to do in randori. This kind of smooth response to a *harai-goshi* attack teaches the fluid motion inherent in the entry and throw of the technique itself. It is also an extremely useful training tool, and as such is one of the best ways to develop good timing. It is done with the standard two-step entry followed by the sweep.

(a)   My opponent and I take standard sleeve/ high collar right-hand grips. He attacks with vigour.

(b)   As he comes out I prepare to move in. I must not move too early, or too late.

(c)   As he regains his position and is about to settle, I am on the way in.

(d)   The throw should be smooth and clean. In *uchikomi* practice, there can be quite a few interchanges before a final throw.

A Rising Opponent Countered by Harai-Goshi (Fig 49)

Keynote
A similar principle is involved; an opponent on his knees can be surprisingly vulnerable to *harai-goshi*, not least because he is not expecting a full-blooded throwing attempt.

(a)   My opponent is on one knee. I do not attempt to pull him up, as this will only make him wary. I let him rise of his own accord.

(b)   When he is half up I can attack, using the most basic entry of all.

(c) and (d)   Once again I can bring my opponent right off the ground.

Morote-Seoi-Nage Countered by Harai-Goshi (Fig 50) (Double Arm Shoulder Throw Countered by Sweeping Hip)

Keynote
This is very useful for contest; in these circumstances, *harai-goshi* can promptly punish a poor attack.

(a)   Uke twists in for a drop shoulder throw but fails to break my balance. I lean on my left hand which acts both as a brake and a hinge.

(b)   I use a little of the impetus created by my partner to bring me round, but as I swing on the hand, my right foot prepares for the larger turn.

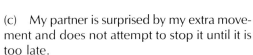

(c)   My partner is surprised by my extra movement and does not attempt to stop it until it is too late.

(d) and (e)   I pull him up sharply, an action which, with the sweep, brings him right off the ground and on to his back.

(f) and (g)   The action from the other side.

Defences

Defence 1 (Fig 51)

Keynote

The safest defence against *harai-goshi* is to stop the attack well before it is truly launched. The aim is to prevent my opponent getting any kind of body contact.

(a) As my opponent turns in, my left hand presses hard against his elbow and sleeve (in this case, I am holding a double lapel grip).

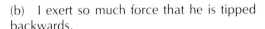

(b) I exert so much force that he is tipped backwards.

(c) I am now in a good position for newaza.

Defence 2: The Tear (Fig 52)

Keynote
Though this does not appear very skilful or positive, it has been used in Japan for decades.

(a)   My opponent builds up for *harai-goshi*.

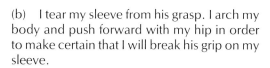

(b)   I tear my sleeve from his grasp. I arch my body and push forward with my hip in order to make certain that I will break his grip on my sleeve.

(c)   My impetus takes me right round.

Training for Harai-Goshi

Harai-goshi is not an easy throw to learn. For a start it makes special demands on balance and general control. Also, as already mentioned, the need to cover quite a lot of ground in front of the opponent, and to establish firm upper body contact, makes tori quite vulnerable to counters. Therefore, considerable preparatory work needs to be done, both alone and with a partner.

As with all judo techniques, the basic feeling of the throw must be absorbed well. The aim is to be able to move in for *harai-goshi* at any time, automatically selecting and adapting the entry to fit the circumstances. The action must be smooth, dynamic and accurate, but it does take time to ingrain the pattern in the body memory.

It is worthwhile starting with a basic stepping pattern on your own before working with a partner. This is one way of clearly distinguishing between the different entries: lateral, spinning or circular. Then it is necessary to add the sweep at the end of a bold movement.

Most of the work is done with one or more partners in standard *uchikomi* practice. However, the *uchikomi* should never be done automatically. It is helpful to give each *uchikomi* set a specific purpose rather than just doing the set mechanically.

Here are some suggestions for particular areas to focus on in separate sets:

1. Stepping patterns. Is accuracy being repeated? Is the movement smooth and rhythmical or still a bit jerky?
2. Hip placement. What kind of hip placement do you want for this particular entry? Is it correct – try drawing uke slightly off his feet to make sure it really is effective. If not, why not?
3. Hand actions and control of the upper body. Experiment with the grips – which grips work for you? Where is the *kuzushi*, i.e. the initial breaking of the balance, coming from – the hand actions or the stepping pattern? Is the basic intention being transmitted to uke? Is uke off-balance when the leg is in a position to sweep?
4. Head action. Is your head still turned

Solo Work

Using the Wall 1 (Fig 53)

Keynote
One of the basic requirements of a good and powerful *harai-goshi* is suppleness in the hip for the sweeping action.

(a)   Stand beside the wall with your standing foot parallel to the wall. Hold on to the wall and sweep, with your foot well pointed and imagining an opponent on the end of it.

(b)   Develop suppleness in a different direction by standing with toes facing the wall, and swinging the leg high.

(c)   Step back slightly and sweep, working on the see-saw effect. When you throw, you need to be able to commit yourself entirely to the throw.

---

towards uke as you start your sweeping action? Do you need a more exaggerated head-turning action?

5.   Sweeping action. Is the action strong and firm, with a straight leg and pointed foot, or is it bent and still just pecking at your partner? Are you well balanced and is your standing leg slightly bent and resilient?

6.   The whole throw. Be aware of the whole throw, from the very start of the movement to the entry into newaza.

Adapt these sets to working on the move, first of all in a one-step pattern with your partner, and then moving more freely around the mat. Experiment to find which entries and which basic movement patterns work best for you.

Get uke to adopt different stances – defensive, upright, acute left or right – and see how you need to adapt to make your throws work.

This is the kind of lively approach that is the basis of the learning process. It is with this alert attitude that a strong *harai-goshi* can be built. Automatic *uchikomi* is largely a waste of time. The following are some specific practices.

Using the Wall 2: Sweeping Practice (Fig 54)

(a)   Step in for the throw.

(b)   Make the turn.

(c)   Start the sweep against the (padded) wall, not too hard, but with a fairly vigorous action. You can develop the feeling of what it is like to work against some resistance.

Hip Placement Practice (Fig 55)

(a)   Step in.

(b)   Make the turn.

(c) and (d)   Bring your hip in against the wall – again, this is to develop a feeling of working against resistance.

Unusual Uchikomi Practices (Fig 56)

Practice 1 (Fig 56)

Keynote
The basic *uchikomi* is done with one other person, but many top fighters work with two people to develop strong and accurate technique. After all, some opponents feel as if they are as strong and as heavy as two people!

(a)   I use just one hand, holding the waist of the back partner. The purpose is to develop effective use of hips and good balance. I just take them off the ground. I must be able to do this balancing comfortably on one leg.

(b)   The exercise seen from the other side.

Practice 2 (Fig 57)

Keynote
This is a practice to develop strong but useful leg muscles.

(a)–(c)   I take my partner on my back. I hold on to the wall and bend my knees. Build up your strength so that you can do a few sets comfortably. Do not forget to do both legs. If you just work on one leg you will end up hobbling around.

Note   When I was competing, and my weight was 103 kilos, I would do a leg press of 500 kilos. So long as you keep flexible and spend most of your time on technical practice, it is helpful to do weights. I used to bench press 205 kilos.

Self-Defence

In France, as in most of Europe, judo is practised by the majority of people as a sport rather than as self-defence, although many actually start judo for self-defence reasons. Certainly, very few competition fighters at national and international level are concerned with judo as a combat weapon in circumstances outside the dojo, unless, perhaps, they are in the police or the army.

I am the same. Yet now, especially as I am no longer a competitor but Technical Director of the French Federation, I am more aware that judo has many aspects, including self-defence.

In fact, I have had two personal experiences in this connection. The first one occurred when I was a young competitor of eighteen and I went to Corsica for a competition. A month before this, I had won the European Espoir Championships, so I felt quite confident.

After the Corsican competition, I spent the evening in a bar in Calvi with some friends from the French team. In the early hours of the morning, there was a misunderstanding and an argument developed. A little later, someone came up to me and asked aggressively, 'What happened with my cousin?' – family feeling is very strong in Corsica. Well, I was European champion, and I felt like the European champion, so when the man threw a punch I blocked it and just naturally threw him with *harai-goshi*. He had no idea what was happening and went flying high into the air and landed heavily.

At that point I realized that it was time to leave the bar. I spent the rest of the night and morning until my plane left more or less in hiding, because cousins in Calvi have many other cousins and a 6ft 4in Frenchman was rather conspicuous.

If it had happened to me ten years later, I would have backed out of the bar rather than cause a fuss, but it left me in no doubt about the usefulness of judo as self-defence.

The second experience happened not so long ago, in France. I had been to a market in Paris with my wife who was pregnant at the time. I was in a car-park, just putting the shopping in the car when a group of around twenty boys approached, acting aggressively. They were only fifteen or sixteen years old, but they were like a pack of jackals out hunting.

This was not the time for conciliatory talk. After a few interchanges, I put down my shopping, stepped into a space, and barked at them in a loud voice, 'Right, let's start. I'll take you one at a time.' They looked at each other for a few seconds and no one stepped forward. Then they faded away.

A lifetime of judo practice does not only teach technique. One absorbs a certain confidence of manner. When you are sure in your mind, it transfers to your actions. I try not to get into trouble, and I never get into fights, but I am never afraid.

Practising Self-Defence

Here are two ways of using *harai-goshi* when wearing ordinary street clothes.

Defence Against a Punch (Fig 58)

(a)   My opponent punches high. I block.

(b)   Immediately, I turn in, bringing my arm around his waist. This is easy against someone who does not know judo, and is not sure of what is coming. Also, it is safer than hoping you can get a good grip from a snatch at his jacket.

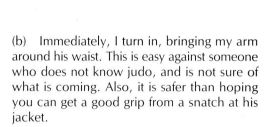

(c)   The block turns to a grip on the sleeve or arm and I turn into position.

(d)   I now bring my opponent off his feet.

(e) and (f)   I throw him on to his back. I do not go down to the ground unless I have to, but most attackers would not quickly get up after a heavy fall like this unless they were trained to breakfall.

79

Defence Against a Grab (Fig 59)

Keynote

These pictures were taken without rehearsal. Francois Fournier, a highly experienced international judo competitor, had no idea what was coming and, despite his experience, even he got a shock from the sheer power of the throw.

(a)   My attacker grabs my shirt.

(b)   I start to attack as if for *ippon-seoi-nage*.

(c)   His position is perfect for a *harai-goshi* action.

(d)   It was at this point that Francois suddenly started to defend. He was not expecting this kind of grip, anymore than if he was a stranger in the street. He started to pull back in earnest, out of natural reaction, but I had grasped his jacket with my right hand.

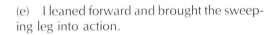

(e)   I leaned forward and brought the sweeping leg into action.

(f)   Look at his shoulder and back muscles. He is trying to pull away from the throw. However, I was able to take him cleanly into the air.

(g)   He was reacting on competition instincts and, having landed very heavily, he immediately started to bridge out and twist, to avoid a newaza follow-up. But there was no referee to say 'Ippon' – except David Finch, the photographer.

Competition Harai-Goshi

Harai-goshi has been seen frequently on the Olympic mat. Anton Geesink, 1964 Olympic Open champion, used *harai-goshi*, although *uchimata* came more frequently. So did his compatriot, Wilhelm Ruska, who won both the heavyweight and Open weight titles in Munich in 1972. In the heavyweight final in Munich he threw Klaus Glahn (West Germany) for ippon with a powerful *harai-goshi*.

Glahn was on the end of another *harai-goshi*, this time in the World Championships in Vienna in 1975. Kazuhiro Ninomiya, the Japanese light-heavyweight, was famous for his *osoto-gari* and, as Glahn also used the throw, he was only too aware of the dangers. Finding himself in the *osoto-gari* position, with Glahn defending strongly, Ninomiya stepped backwards and switched to a forward direction, throwing with a powerful *harai-goshi*. It was a classic exchange, one that is seen regularly in contest, in fact as frequently as *harai-goshi* is executed as a direct attack.

Harai-goshi has not been the preserve of the tall man. Sumio Endo, who stood only 5ft

6in, threw the 6ft Russian, Vladimir Kuznetsov, for ippon in the Open weight final of the World Championships in Paris in 1979 with *harai-makikomi* – it was the only technique in the match.

The 1980s generally saw a diminishing use of *harai-goshi*, partly, perhaps, because of the widespread adoption of tailored jackets which made grip-breaking relatively easy. Another important factor was the increasing use of pick-ups in defense – and not just by the Russians. The dual problems of getting the standing leg into position, and the danger of stretching a leg across the opponent seemed to present too many difficulties at the highest level of competition.

However, the closing years of the decade saw some extraordinary examples which shows that, while fashion may have put it on the sidelines a little, it is still an immensely powerful technique.

One of the most dramatic weight categories of the 1988 Olympics in Seoul was the men's light-heavyweight, and notably the final

Olympic appearance of the superb campaigner, Belgium's Robert van de Walle. He was then thirty-four and, everyone was sure, well past his best. But he defied age and expectations by beating the 1984 Olympic champion, Hyung-Zoo Ha (South Korea) and then the Soviet Union's Vitaly Poddubny. Just as it seemed van de Walle would cruise his way to the final, he was caught by a spectacular *okuri-ashi-barai* for ippon by the West German, Marc Meiling.

Van de Walle should have been mentally crushed by that defeat. Instead, he came back through the repêchage with a determination that made him one of the outstanding players of the event, even though he only won a bronze.

He took hold of Jacek Beutler (Poland) who was no mean opposition, thundered past his defence, and levelled him with *harai-goshi*. It was possible to see Beutler visibly crumble under the attack. The Belgian followed that with another ippon, this time using *harai-makikomi* against the American Robert Berland (who had won a silver medal in the 1984 Olympics, at middleweight). Once again, Berland could offer no defence against the total commitment of van de Walle's attack.

Harai-goshi was a throw used by van de Walle throughout his long and distinguished career, and it was significant that it was still there, as sharp and as dangerous as ever, in the last years. (Van de Walle retired after Seoul, then came back a year later and won a bronze medal at the world championships in Belgrade where he used *harai-goshi* again.)

Among the most decisive individual throws in the 1990 European Championships was *harai-goshi*, again used by a light-heavyweight. Stephane Traineau (France) received something of a shock when he was thrown for waza-ari by an unknown Greek, Nikas. He got up, eyes afire, took hold of the Greek's belt, and absolutely buried him with *harai-goshi*. Only then did he look towards his French team-mates and break into a smile.

However much it might have been slightly at the mercy of fashion at the top level of competition, *harai-goshi* has never lost its popularity in dojos throughout the world, and the return to bigger jackets in the 1990s is expected to foster a return of *harai-goshi* to the main arena of competitive judo.

Fig 60(a) and (b)   One of the most classic *harai-goshi* techniques ever photographed in contest. Guy Auffray (France) throws Hansen (Denmark) in the 1975 World Championships in Vienna.

Fig 61   In the final of the light heavyweight category in the 1975 World Championships in Vienna, I attacked Ishibashi (Japan) with *harai-goshi* and, while it unbalanced him, it did not quite work.

Fig 62 (a)   A later attack on Ishibashi did work. I was trying to control my right arm – one of the main defences against *harai-goshi* – but instead of reaching for his jacket, I slipped my hand over his head. I was already in position for *harai-makikomi,* with my foot hooked in and my head low.

(b)   My turn is complete. Ishibashi is weighted on his right leg, and tries to stop the technique in its tracks by bringing his left arm around my waist.

(c) But this does not stop the turn as this photograph shows so graphically. Ishibashi is taken right up in the air. The referee, whose moustache is even more magnificent than mine, looks on in expectation.

(d) I continue the rotation – so important in a *harai-makikomi* of this nature – as I drive for the mat.

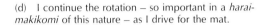

(e) I do not have much of Ishibashi's right arm to control, and the Japanese nearly manages to prevent even a part-score.

(f) But my final twist clinches it – yuko.

Fig 63 (a)   Margaret Castro (USA) is extremely tall and used her height effectively in winning a bronze at the World Championships in Vienna in 1984. She positioned herself perfectly for the attack, pulling her opponent high and on to the right foot.

(b)   Pulling up with the right arm, elbow pointed – a characteristic movement for a tall fighter – to increase the lift, she sweeps easily.

(c)   Her opponent tries to defend by putting an arm around Castro's waist, prompting the American to switch to *harai-makikomi.*

(d)   The result is that her opponent overspins, and thus only concedes a yuko.

Fig 64 (a)   The real sweeping action can be seen here as Gunther Neureuther (West Germany) sweeps Koba Kurtanidze (Soviet Union) off his feet in the final of the Tournoi de Paris, 1980.

(b)   Then Neureuther drives to the side . . .

(c)   . . . and achieves ippon with the help of the upper body rotation.

Fig 65 (a)   Tengiz Khouboulouri (Soviet Union) throws Robert van de Walle (Belgian) the Olympic light heavyweight champion, with *harai-goshi* for yuko to win the European Championships in Debrecen, Hungary. Note the belt grip taken with the right arm.

(b)   The effect of the grip is to take van de Walle down to the floor almost completely on his back. Only at the last second, after this shot was taken, did the Belgian twist to prevent the ippon.

Fig 66   Paul Radburn (Britain) throws Mihail Cioc (Romania) with *harai-goshi* in the Moscow Olympics, 1980. He has lost the sleeve grip, but the arm-over-the-back grip and the good sweeping action of the leg managed to turn the attack into a score.

Fig 67 (a)–(d)   A classic example of *hidari-ashi-guruma* performed by my compatriot Angelo Parisi on no less a figure than Sergei Novikov (Soviet Union) in the 1980 European Championships in Vienna.

(a)   Holding lapel/armpit grips, Angelo twists in with the classic spinning entry and the smooth accuracy of his movement has already put most of Novikov's weight on his left foot.

(b)   The next stage, as Angelo, looking towards the spot on the mat where he intends to land Novikov, unbalances the Russian totally.

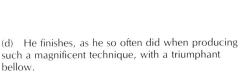

(c)   As he projects Novikov down to the ground, his left foot settles into a *tai-otoshi* position. Note the perfect control of his hands.

(d)   He finishes, as he so often did when producing such a magnificent technique, with a triumphant bellow.

Fig 68 (a) Grigory Veritchev, the Soviet heavyweight, on his way to a bronze medal in the European Championships in Belgrade, 1986. He has achieved the first goal of *harai-goshi*, i.e. putting his opponent's weight on to the right foot.

(b) His opponent, Mihail Cioc (Romania) cannot stop being turned.

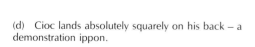

(c) Veritchev drives down to the mat.

(d) Cioc lands absolutely squarely on his back – a demonstration ippon.

Fig 69 (a)   Motta (Italy) attacked Blair (UK) with this well-controlled *harai-goshi*. At first Blair must have felt that he had it under control, because he had twisted away from the throw.

(b)   But Motta's control with the hands, and his balance, was sufficiently strong to bring Blair back on to the throw. Note the effective lift-pull action with the right hand and the pulling-turning action with his left hand. Blair is still trying to defend by pushing away with his left hand.

(c) and (d)   Blair had been pulled right round. Motta's hands are still actively working, making this very much a hand throw, and they take Blair right down to the ground.

Fig 70 (a)–(d)   Grigory Veritchev (Soviet Union) used *harai-goshi* frequently through his reign as one of the top heavyweights in the 1980s. Here he throws Turkey's Metin Orgarun with a superb *harai-goshi* on his way to winning the world title in Essen in 1987.

Fig 71 (a) Britain's Peter Donnelly attacks Jorgen Rothlisberger (Switzerland) with *harai-goshi/tsuri-komi-goshi* in the 1979 World Championships in Paris. However, the canny Swiss, who the following year was to take the Olympic title, executes the required defence – grip breaking.

(b) In later action from the same fight, Rothlisberger attacked Donnelly with *harai-goshi*, but he has neither the balance nor the control.

Fig 73 Four years after winning the world title, I was still doing harai-goshi – here, against Peter Kostenberger (Austria), at the Tournoi de Paris, 1979.

Fig 74 Portly Dimitar Zaprianov produces an ingenious defence against Willie Wilhelm (Austria) in the 1984 European Championships in Liege. Not only did he sink his (considerable) weight, but he very cleverly inserted his left toe in the Austrian's trouser leg, thus managing to pin both firmly to the ground. This kind of defence is only available to martial artists of the highest calibre and is not to be relied upon by those who are not advanced adepts. But was it luck?

Fig 75 (a)–(f)   Robert van de Walle (Belgium) used *harai-goshi* in all his repêchage fights for his bronze medal at the 1988 Olympics. But few were as spectacular as this, against Poland's Jacek Beutler. It started as a pure hip technique, but as Beutler tried to step around, van de Walle switched to *harai-goshi* with devastating effect.

Index